ANIMALS HAVE JOBS TOO!

By: Alexandra Leigh Numeroff

Illustrated By: Eminence System

Inspired By: Claire Kelly

Printed by IngramSpark, in the United States of America.

Illustrated by Eminence System.

ISBN Number: 978-1-0878-5671-1

In loving memory of my dear friend Falon Morris and to my friends and family. Without you all, this book would not be possible. I would also like to dedicate this book to my students for being my biggest supporters.

Hello! I'm your librarian.
My name is Sue!
I'm a bookworm and
I would like to teach you.

Today you're going to learn
About what my friends do.
Humans don't realize that
We have jobs too!

You're going to get clues
From each of my crew.
Try to guess who they are
And the jobs that they do!

Get ready to listen
You're in for a treat
Because these interesting animals
Are a pleasure to meet!

My name is **COLBY**.
I chase mice away.
If I can't catch them
I go off and play.

Leave the rodents to me.
I have them under control.
Get rid of your traps.
Call me mouse patrol.

Who am I?
What's my job?

COLBY THE CAT

I'M AN EXTERMINATOR!

My name is **BONNIE**.
When I fly, I feel free.
I pollinate flowers
And make honey.

My honey is sweet.
It's perfect with your treat.
Come sit down
I'll make you something
Yummy to eat.

Who am I?
What's my job?

BONNIE THE BEE

I'M A BAKER!

My name is **ROCKY**.
I take your trash.
If I were human
I'd get rewarded with cash.

I come out at night
Dark circles under my eyes.
Rummaging through garbage
To find a surprise.

Who am I?
What's my job?

ROCKY THE RACCOON

I'M A SANITATION WORKER!

My name is **CAMI**.
I change colors.
I can blend in with anything.
I'm not like the others.

I can sneak up on enemies
Without being seen.
I'm like the FBI.
You'll want me on your team!

Who am I?
What's my job?

CAMI THE CHAMELEON

I'M A SPY!

My name is **DAISY.**
I help lead the blind.
Anything they need
I will surely find.

When my best friend
Is going through strife
I'm always here to help him
And even save his life!

Who am I?
What's my job?

DAISY THE SERVICE DOG

I'M A NURSE!

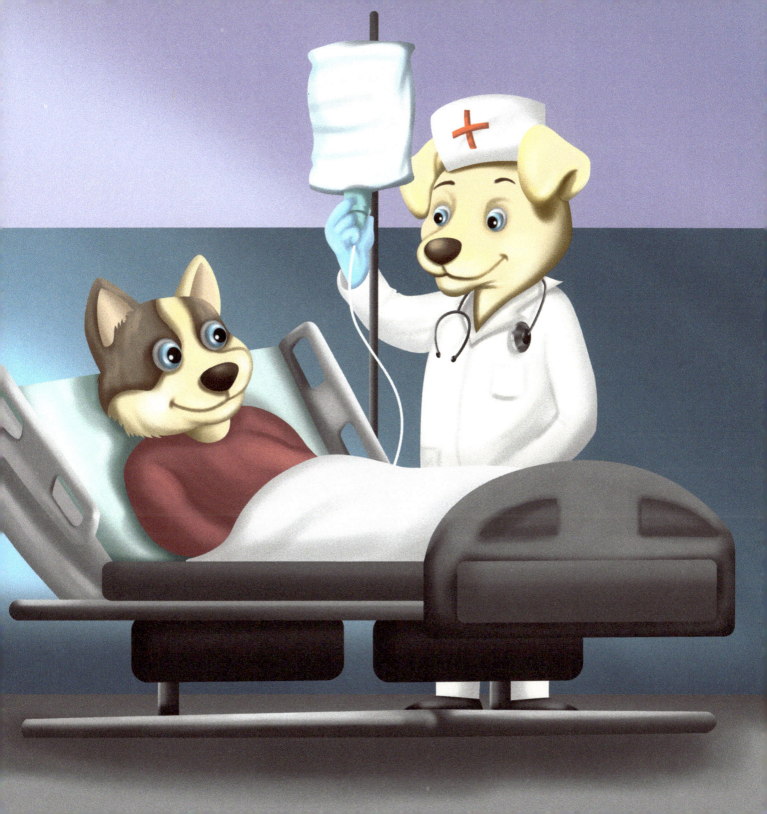

My name is **HENRY**.
I have a long mane.
All of my friends
Think it's insane.

I eat lots of hay and
Back in the day
I would pull you in a carriage
And take you away.

A basketball game is
Named after me.
But racing on TV
Is where I shine
You'll see!

Who am I?
What's my job?

HENRY THE HORSE

I'M A TRACK STAR!

My name is **MARTY**.
I swing from trees.
I eat lots of bananas
Filled with vitamin C.

I could assist with daily tasks
And pick up what you drop.
I can even press buttons
So hand me your laptop.

Who am I?
What's my job?

MARTY THE MONKEY

I'M AN ASSISTANT!

My name is **CHRISTIE**.
I have humps on my back.
Let's go, come on board.
Bring your backpack!

I can take you anywhere.
It'll be a fun ride.
I was born in the desert
Where it's dry outside!

Who am I?
What's my job?

CHRISTIE THE CAMEL

I'M A BUS DRIVER!

My name is **DANNY**.
Watch me flip in the sea.
I use sonar to detect objects
That are far away from me.

I only communicate
In high frequency.
I love to solve mysteries
And I'm smart as can be.

Who am I?
What's my job?

DANNY THE DOLPHIN

I'M A DETECTIVE!

My name is **BILLY**
And I build dams a lot.
I protect my home
Using whatever I've got.

I'm like a lumberjack
Combined with a carpenter.
I have a big tail and
My body is covered in fur.

Who am I?
What's my job?

BILLY THE BEAVER

I'M A BUILDER!

My name is **PENNY**.
I'm so colorful.
Look at my feathers
They are beautiful!

Strutting down the runway
Like the belle that I am.
I was born to do this
Because I'm very glam!

Who am I?
What's my job?

PENNY THE PEACOCK

I'M A MODEL!

My name is **SALLY**.
I spin again and again.
To make a web from silk
That comes from my abdomen.

My webs have designs
And lots of patterns too.
Just hand me some thread.
I can make something for you!

Who am I?
What's my job?

SALLY THE SPIDER

I'M A WEAVER!

My name is **WALLY**.
I love banging my beak.
When heard from a distance
Many mates I do meet.

They call me the drummer
As I have a constant beat.
Sometimes it's loud
And you could hear me
From the street!

Who am I?
What's my job?

WALLY THE WOODPECKER

I'M A MUSICIAN!

My name is **EDDIE**.
I create electricity.
Up to 600 volts
Flow through my body.

I may shock you.
That's how I stun my prey.
If you see me in the water
You should surely swim away!

Who am I?
What's my job?

EDDIE THE ELECTRIC EEL

I'M AN ELECTRICIAN!

My name is **RANDY**.
There's no fur on my tail.
When humans see me running
Their faces turn pale.

I go underground
Where it is so dark.
Sniffing for explosives
It's no walk in the park.

Who am I?
What's my job?

RANDY THE RAT

I'M IN THE BOMB SQUAD!

So you met all my friends.
What do you think of them now?
Hardworking and
busy I know,
Holy cow!

There's a whole
Separate world
That you don't
know about.

Just keep studying
Animals and then
You'll find out!

Appendix

Did You Know

	• Europe introduced cats into the Americas as a form of pest control in the 1750s. • Despite popular belief, many cats are actually lactose intolerant. • 200 feral cats prowl the park at Disneyland doing their part to control rodents — the ones who don't wear funny outfits and speak in squeaky voices.
	• All worker bees are female. • A bee produces a teaspoon of honey in her lifetime. • To produce a kilogram of honey, bees fly the equivalent of three times around the world in air miles. • The type of flower the bees take their nectar from determines the honey's flavor.
	• The raccoon's black fur under their eyes help them see more clearly. • While most animals use either sight, sound, or smell to hunt, raccoons rely on their sense of touch to locate goodies. • "Dousing" is a behavior utilized by raccoons to stimulate their sense of

	touch. For humans, this can appear like they're washing their food.
	• Chameleons change their colors for a number of reasons such as: poor health, pregnancy, exposure to light and temperature changes, if they feel threatened, and mating. • Although it's commonly believed that these animals can match their environment's colors, they can only do so in certain circumstances. For instance, they cannot match patterns or colors found in printed clothes.

- Guide dogs learn to stop at curbs and stairs, move around obstacles and sometimes to respond to simple commands like "Find the chair."
- Just like humans, guide dogs eventually retire — usually after roughly eight to 10 years of service.
- Labradors, Golden Retrievers, and German Shepherds are the most common guide dog breeds.

- Horses gallop at around 27 mph.
- The fastest recorded sprinting speed of a horse was 55 mph. Even the fastest humans can only run about 28 mph.
- Horses have bigger eyes than any other mammal that lives on land.
- Horses can sleep both standing up and lying down.

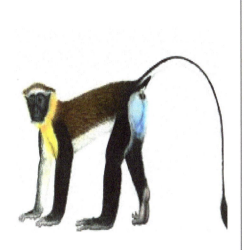

- A monkey helper can assist with various tasks such as retrieving dropped or out of reach items, helping with a drink of coffee, scratching itches, pushing buttons and switches for remotes, phones, computers, etc.
- Monkeys can peel fruits, they can pick up objects, and they use the thumbs for grooming.
- Capuchin monkeys were the first primates to use highly skilled tools in the wild. Archaeological studies revealed that the animals have been using stone tools for thousands of years.

- Camels, like donkeys, have been used as a method of transportation for humans for a very long time – thousands of years, believe it or not.
- These sturdy and strong animals can carry up to 500 pounds on their backs, so people or goods can be transported.
- The camel's hump is actually very useful. It consists of stored fat which the camels can resource when food and water are very limited.

- Dolphins have developed the ability to use echolocation, often known as sonar, to help them see better underwater. Echolocation allows dolphins to "see" by interpreting the echoes of sound waves that bounce off of objects near them in the water.
- To echolocate objects nearby, dolphins produce high-frequency clicks. These clicks create sound waves that travel quickly through the water around them.

- Beavers build dams which are made of reeds, sticks, and branches. They are built to slow down the erosion of streams and provide new habitats for aquatic life.
- Beavers don't just build dams. They also build lodges which is typically built with an air hole in its roof to allow ventilation. The floor is typically covered in wood shavings to absorb the moisture.

	• Beavers are the largest rodents in North America!
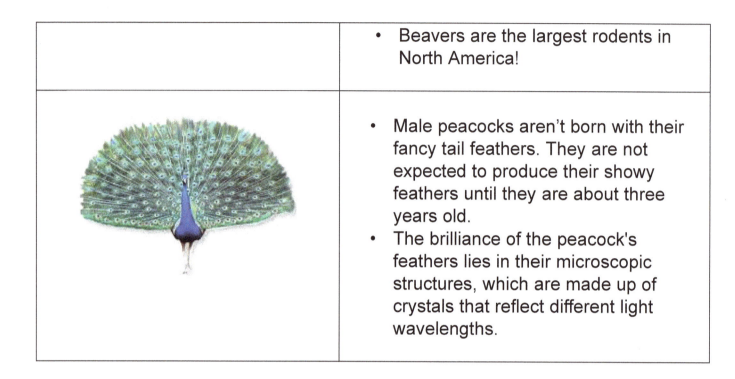	• Male peacocks aren't born with their fancy tail feathers. They are not expected to produce their showy feathers until they are about three years old. • The brilliance of the peacock's feathers lies in their microscopic structures, which are made up of crystals that reflect different light wavelengths.

	• One spider can create up to seven different types of webs, each of which is used for a different purpose. Each web is different and consumes a large amount of energy to generate. • Some spiders, known as the "orb weavers", set the framework and radial threads for the web using dragline silk. The silk is then applied to the top layer using a glue-like substance. The web takes about an hour to build.
	• In the animal world, the bird kingdom is full of woodpeckers, who are the only creatures that can make a sound with a non-body part. They do it to attract mates, to locate food, and communicate with other animals. • Woodpeckers drum on a variety of objects to communicate territory as well as to exercise and play.

	• Electric eels have thousands of cells that produce electricity. They can produce a 5x stronger electric shock than the standard US wall socket. • The electric eel's front half of its body is full of cells. The other half is empty and acts like tiny batteries. • Electric eels can't see what they're shocking. They're mostly blind and use a radar-like system of electrical pulses to navigate and find food.
	• Rats have such a good sense of smell, they have been used to detect landmines and diagnose diseases such as tuberculosis. • These rats are trained to detect the presence of a chemical compound inside an explosive. They then scratch the top of the explosive to alert their human co–workers. • In the dark, rats use their whiskers to identify objects. They can also tell the shape of objects and orientation of them by looking at them in different colors.

Works Cited

"101 Amazing Cat Facts: Fun Trivia about Your Feline Friend in Charlottesville, VA." *Charlottesville Cat Care Clinic*, 5 July 2018, https://cvillecatcare.com/veterinary-topics/101-amazing-cat-facts-fun-trivia-about-your-feline-friend/.

"50 Cat Facts You Probably Didn't Know." *Georgia Veterinary Associates*, 4 Nov. 2021, https://www.mygavet.com/services/blog/50-cat-facts-you-probably-didnt-know.

"8 Facts to Celebrate International Beaver Day." *Smithsonian's National Zoo*, 5 Apr. 2019, https://nationalzoo.si.edu/animals/news/8-facts-celebrate-international-beaver-day.

Automatic Trap Company. "101 Amazing Facts about Rats." *Automatic Trap Company*, https://www.automatictrap.com/pages/101-rat-facts.

"Bees – Fun Facts." *Science Learning Hub*, https://www.sciencelearn.org.nz/resources/2002-bees-fun-facts.

Debczak, Michele. "10 Clever Facts about Raccoons." *Mental Floss*, Mental Floss, 29 Jan. 2018, https://www.mentalfloss.com/article/527175/10-clever-facts-about-raccoons.

Drake, Amber L. "18 Fun and Compelling Chameleon Facts ." *LoveToKnow*, LoveToKnow Media, 7 Oct. 2021, https://small-pets.lovetoknow.com/reptiles-amphibians/chameleon-facts.

"Fun Camel Facts for Kids." *Cool Kid Facts*, 26 Dec. 2021, https://www.coolkidfacts.com/camel-facts-for-kids/.

"Fun Facts about Seeing Eye Dogs." *The Seeing Eye - Fun Facts about Seeing Eye Dogs.*, https://www.seeingeye.org/blog/fun-facts-about-seeing-eye.html.

"Fun Horse Facts for Kids - Interesting Information about Horses." *Science Kids - Fun Science & Technology for Kids!*, https://www.sciencekids.co.nz/sciencefacts/animals/horse.html.

"How Do Dolphins Use Echolocation?" *Wonderopolis*, https://www.wonderopolis.org/wonder/how-do-dolphins-use-echolocation.

Kiley. *Dickinson County Conservation Board*, 19 Aug. 2020, https://dickinsoncountyconservationboard.com/2018/10/10/nine-fun-facts-about-woodpeckers/.

Leach, Nicola. "Fun Fact Friday: Spider Web Fun Facts." *Alliance Work Partners*, 9 Sept. 2021, https://www.awpnow.com/main/2019/06/21/fun-fact-friday-spider-web-fun-facts/.

Leary, Catie. "11 Fascinating Facts about Monkeys." *Treehugger*, https://www.treehugger.com/things-you-didnt-know-about-monkeys-4869728.

Mag, The. "9 Shocking Facts about Electric Eels." *Mental Floss*, Mental Floss, 30 May 2015, https://www.mentalfloss.com/article/63244/9-shocking-facts-about-electric-eels.

"Magawa the Hero Rat Retires from Job Detecting Landmines." *BBC News*, BBC, 4 June 2021, https://www.bbc.com/news/world-asia 57345703#:~:text=The%20rats%20are%20trained%20to,alert%20their%20human%20co%2Dworkers.

Six Surprising Facts about Spiderwebs - JSTOR DAILY. https://daily.jstor.org/surprising-facts-about-spiderwebs/.

"Woof! 9 Interesting - and Surprising - Facts about Guide Dogs." *Perkins School for the Blind*, 8 Mar. 2022, https://www.perkins.org/woof-9-interesting-and-surprising-facts-about-guide-dogs/.

CPSIA information can be obtained
at www.ICGtesting.com
Printed in the USA
BVHW020843010722
641019BV00020B/81